The Adventure Begins

To my students:
Always remember you have
the chance to make the world a
better place! Even the smallest
ideas can lead to big changes.

Published in association with Bear With Us Productions

©2020 Brittany Plumeri
The right of Brittany Plumeri as the author of this work has been asserted by her in accordance with the Copyright Designs and Patents Act 1988.

All rights reserved, including the right of reproduction in whole or part in any form.

Written By
Brittany Plumeri

The Adventure Begins

Illustrated By
Johanna Zverzina

The Isles of Mer

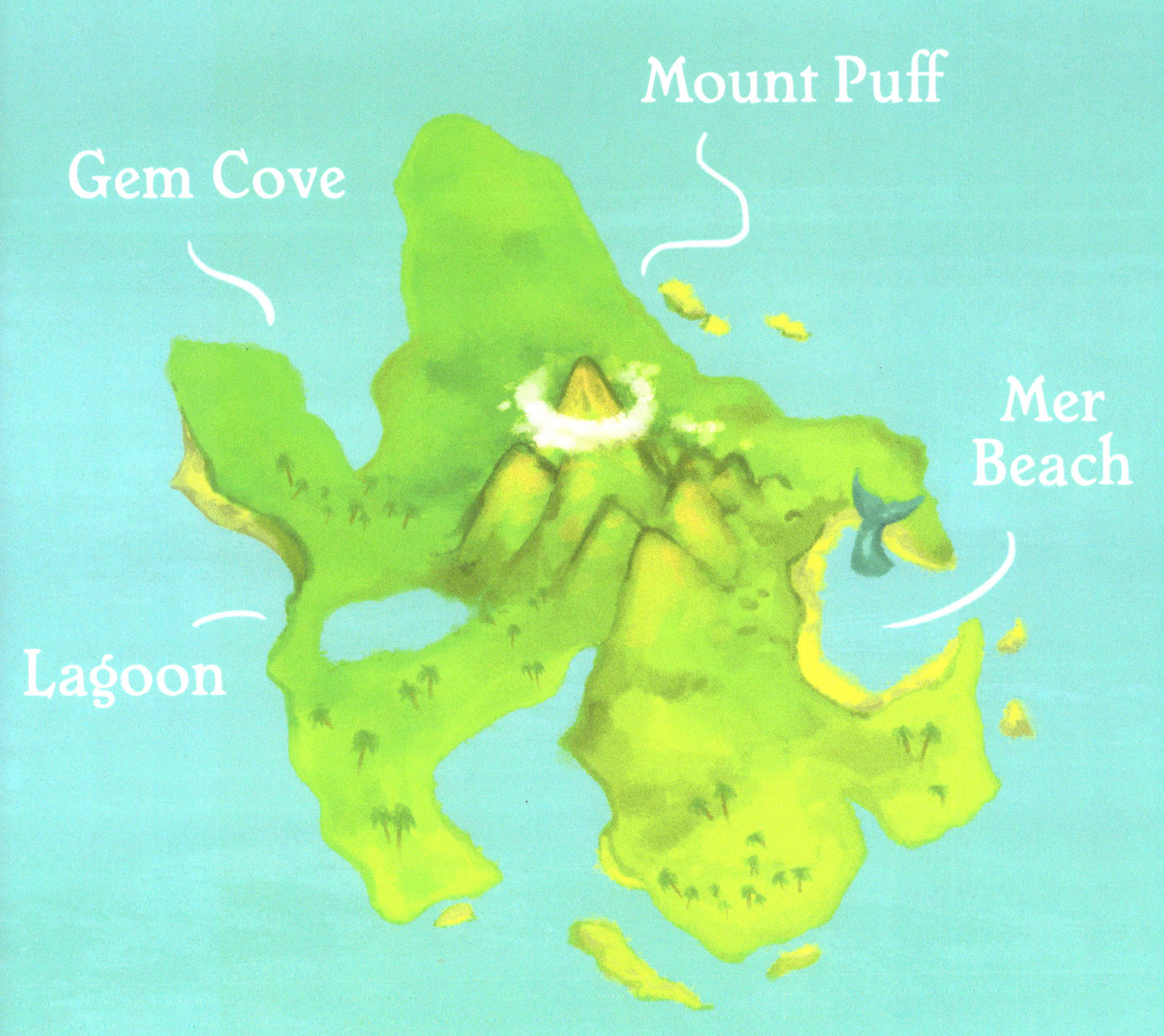

I know of a place
where adventures occur.

It's out on the seas called
The Isles of Mer.

The Island has treasures and
creatures to meet,
like Merzzlings, whose height
measures only two feet.

Be careful!
For if you forget to be kind,
these mischievous creatures
will surely remind

and bring you to Mer,
where I'm happy to bet

they'll teach you a lesson you won't soon forget.

And that's just what happened
to one particular child,
a young boy named Noah,
who was recklessly wild.

Back on the island, the Merzzlings all met,
and were anxiously reading the Merzzling Gazette,
which reported a story about this young lad,
and the fact that he treated his classmates so bad.
They all shook their heads as they read the news copy,
"I know what to do!"
said a Merzzling named Floppy.

A big puff of smoke!
Floppy held up his hand,
then, POOF!
Noah promptly appeared in the sand.

While turning around
in confusion and shock,
the boy spotted Floppy
on top of a rock.

The Merzzling told Noah
he needed his help.
Miss Hoon hid his gem
deep in the kelp.

"I'll help!" Noah said, which put Floppy at ease. They went up a mountain, all covered in trees.

While climbing that mountain, poor Floppy did huff. Noah said, "You huff much too much, ball of Fluff!"

But Floppy ignored him and just kept on going.
Now it was Noah whose weakness was showing.
While huffing and puffing, they got to the top,
but Noah was panting, "I just need to stop!"

Then Floppy did stop, and he sat on a rock.
But Noah was puzzled:
"Why didn't he mock?"
Descending again down the other side's end,
Floppy led Noah around a cliff bend.

From out of the bushes
a tree branch stuck out,
and WHACK!
It smacked Floppy
on top of his snout!

How Noah did laugh
while he watched this ordeal,
but cried out in pain
when a branch whacked his heel.

His tune quickly changed,
and *he* started to cry.
Then Floppy showed up with a leaf for his eye.
And Noah was thinking,
"This Merzzling's so nice,
although I have mocked him,
and more than just twice."

They trekked down the mountain
and heard a loud laughter for there sat
Miss Hoon —
just the one they were after!

She said to the Merzzling, "You're surely a pest!
I've stolen one gem; now I'll take all the rest!"
Then Noah's face reddened. He felt really mad.
"Don't dare make this kind-hearted Merzzling feel sad!"

Miss Hoon asked him then,
"Did I tell you to speak?"
And for the first time,
Noah felt somewhat meek.

The boy could now see that Miss Hoon was quite mean. This made him remember his morning routine.

Each day he would pick on a classmate or two.
But now he could tell what's the right thing to do.
He answered Miss Hoon, "I deserve this, I do.
I tend to behave exactly like you."
"My parents, my siblings, my teachers, my peers...
They're far from deserving my terrible sneers."

The Merzzlings popped out, and they started to shout,
"You did it Noah! You've figured it out!"
Miss Hoon glanced at Noah and gave him a smile,
which showed she'd been in on the plan,
all the while.

Then just like that,
there was a bright flash,
and Noah was back in his room
with a CRASH!

From that day forward,
Noah would recall,
Floppy and how kindness is the key after all.

www.ingramcontent.com/pod-product-compliance
Lightning Source LLC
Chambersburg PA
CBHW042030100526
44587CB00029B/4353